W9-AMA-456

The FBI

Federal Bureau of Investigation

TRISTAN BOYER BINNS

Heinemann Library
Chicago, Illinois

© 2003 Reed Educational & Professional Publishing
Published by Heinemann Library,
an imprint of Reed Educational & Professional Publishing,
Chicago, IL

Customer Service 888-454-2279

Visit our website at www.heinemannlibrary.com

All rights reserved. No part of this publication may be
reproduced or transmitted in any form or by any means,
electronic or mechanical, including photocopying,
recording, taping, or any information storage and retrieval
system, without permission in writing from the publisher.

Page Layout by Molly Heron
Printed and bound in the United States
by Lake Book Manufacturing

07 06 05 04 03
10 9 8 7 6 5 4 3 2 1

Library of Congress Cataloging-in-Publication Data
Binns, Tristan Boyer, 1968-
   FBI: Federal Bureau of Investigation / Tristan Boyer
Binns.
      p. cm. -- (Government agencies)
Includes index.
Summary: An introduction to the Federal Bureau of
Investigation,
discussing its nature, structure, and responsibilities.
   ISBN 1-58810-499-0 (HC) 1-58810-983-6 (Pbk)
   1. United States. Federal Bureau of Investigation--Juvenile
literature. 2. Criminal investigation--United States--
Juvenile
literature. [1. United States. Federal Bureau of
Investigation.] I.
Title. II. Series.
HV8144.F43 B54 2002
63.25'068--dc21

                          2001005953

Acknowledgments
Cover photograph by Robert Maass/Corbis
p. 4 Reuters/Chief Brandon Brewer/U.S. Coast
Guard/TimePix; pp. 5, 14C, 22L, 23, 24, 25, 30, 31B, 33,
38, 39, 42, 43T Tristan Boyer Binns/Heinemann Library;
p. 7L Jack Manning/New York Times Co./Archive Photos;
pp. 7R, 9, 14B, 20R, 21, 22R, 28B, 29, 34, 35, 36, 37, 40,
41T Courtesy of the Federal Bureau of Investigation; pp.
10T, 13L Bettmann/Corbis; pp. 10B, 12, 13R AP Photos;
p. 11 New York Times Co./Archive Photos; p. 14T Jay
Mallin Photos; pp. 15T, 15B, 19 Media Archive/U.S.
Department of State; pp. 15C, 16, 17T, 27B, 43B Robert
Lifson/Heinemann Library; p. 17B Stan Wayman/TimePix;
p. 18 Dave Caulkin/AP Photos; p. 20L Robert
Maass/Corbis; pp. 26, 27T Getty Images; p. 28T Anna
Clopet/Corbis; p. 31TL Stone/Getty Images, Inc. p. 31TR
Frank Lane Picture Agency/Corbis; p. 41B Galen
Rowell/Corbis

Every effort has been made to contact copyright holders of
any material reproduced in this book. Any omissions will
be rectified in subsequent printings if notice is given to the
publisher.

The author and publisher would like to thank the following
people for their help in the preparation of this book:
Dr. Kate Theisen, Mary Lou Leitner, Karen Lanning,
Andreas Stephens, Kenny Neu, Bob Fram, Kurt Crawford,
and Bobi Wallace at FBI Headquarters in Washington,
D.C.; Sarah Perlman; Special Agent Ross Rice at FBI
Chicago.

Special thanks to Neil Schiff in the Office of Public and
Congressional Affairs —FBIHQ, Washington, for his
interest in and enthusiasm for this project.

Note to the Reader: Some words are shown in
bold, **like this.** You can find out what they mean
by looking in the glossary.

Contents

To Uphold the Law

Many people find crime investigations exciting. They like putting together facts and **evidence** to solve crimes. But **investigating** and solving crimes is also about working for **justice**.

In the United States, many people work for justice. These include local and state police officers, judges, and the Department of Justice, or DOJ, in Washington, D.C. The person in charge of the DOJ is the attorney general—the top lawyer in the United States. It is the attorney general's job to **prosecute** crimes against the United States. The attorney general gets help from the **Federal** Bureau of Investigation, or FBI.

Fighting Terrorism

Terrorists attacked the United States on September 11, 2001. They **hijacked** four airplanes and crashed them into the World Trade Center in New York City, into the Pentagon (the U.S. armed forces headquarters just outside Washington, D.C.), and into an empty field in Pennsylvania. Thousands of people at more than 32 **government agencies** jumped into action. The FBI is the lead agency when the United States investigates acts of terrorism. More than 4,000 FBI special agents and 3,000 professional support workers with the FBI went to work. This included more than 100 FBI Laboratory experts in explosives, **DNA,** trace evidence, chemistry, and other areas. They went to New York, the Pentagon, and to Pennsylvania to search for and **analyze** evidence.

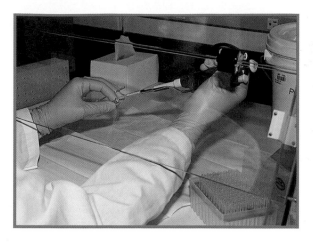

FBI lab workers can test very small bits of hair or blood. They can figure out who the samples belong to.

People must learn many new skills to become FBI special agents. One example is firing a gun.

Some people **commit** crimes within a small area, like a town. The criminals stay or live nearby. In these types of crimes, the town's police work to catch the criminals. Other criminals work in large areas, across many towns or states. Their crimes are called "crimes against the United States." The FBI works to solve these types of crimes. The information the FBI discovers is given to the DOJ. The FBI investigates other crimes as well. It investigates people who want to attack the U.S. through terrorism, or who want to find out U.S. secrets.

The FBI has science laboratories, or labs, to help investigate many types of crimes. FBI scientists can identify people from fingerprints. They can tell what kind of gun was fired by looking at bullets. They can look at videotapes to figure out how fast cars were moving before accidents. All these tools help to solve crimes.

Mission Statement

"The Mission of the FBI is to uphold the law through the investigation of violations of federal criminal law; to protect the United States from foreign **intelligence** and terrorist activities; to provide leadership and **law enforcement** assistance to federal, state, local, and international agencies; and to perform these responsibilities in a manner that is responsive to the needs of the public and is faithful to the Constitution of the United States."

Investigations

The FBI is divided into seven main programs. Each of these **investigates** a special type of crime.

The Programs

- **VIOLENT CRIMES AND MAJOR OFFENDERS PROGRAM**

This program handles crimes in which people are threatened, hurt, or killed. Some of these crimes are kidnapping, **blackmail,** bank robbery, and murder.

- **WHITE-COLLAR CRIME PROGRAM**

This program investigates crimes in which people are not physically hurt. Some examples are **fraud,** cheating with money or in elections, and destroying the environment.

- **ORGANIZED CRIME/DRUG PROGRAM**

This program investigates crimes **committed** by groups or organizations. Both **organized crime** and drug dealing need many people to make them work, so the same FBI program looks into these two types.

- **CIVIL RIGHTS PROGRAM**

This program helps **enforce** the laws that protect the rights of all Americans. Agents handle problems of **discrimination** against people because of their sex or the color of their skin.

- **DOMESTIC TERRORISM PROGRAM**

This program tries to stop people from hurting people or damaging buildings in the United States.

- **NATIONAL FOREIGN INTELLIGENCE PROGRAM**

This program tries to keep all foreign spies from stealing U.S. government and military secrets. Agents here also stop criminals from damaging banking and transportation systems.

- **APPLICANT PROGRAM**

This program investigates people who have important jobs in the United States government. Workers here try to make sure that all U.S. government workers are honest, can be trusted, and will not be **security risks.**

Carlo Gambino was suspected of being a leader in the **Mafia**—an organized crime group. He was arrested by FBI special agents in 1970.

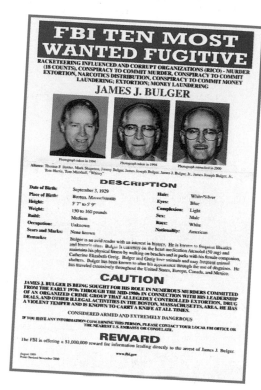

Each person on the FBI Ten Most Wanted **Fugitives** list is on a flier. It contains a description of the person's crimes and a picture.

Sometimes, **high-tech** devices such as telephone **bugs** are used to get information. Other times, special agents go **undercover** to get information. Every division helps. The divisions' expert services include **analyzing evidence,** collecting information, and training special agents.

Know It

In 1998, computer **hackers** electronically entered top-secret U.S. Air Force and Navy computers. At first, the government thought the hackers were spies or **terrorists.** The FBI helped find the hackers who really did it—and they were teenagers!

You Can Help

The FBI started its Ten Most Wanted Fugitives program more than 50 years ago. It shows pictures and tells the stories of people who have not been caught. The fliers ask citizens to tell the FBI if they have seen a fugitive. Out of the 467 people shown, 438 have been found. Citizens helped find 140 of them.

How the FBI Began

When the United States were first created, most Americans were proud to be part of the new country. But they took most of their laws and leadership from their cities and states. The main government of the country, called the **federal** government, was much less important. It was simply too difficult to govern large areas from a distant city. Transportation was slow and difficult. Mail service took a long time. Before the telegraph and telephone were invented, even news took a long time to spread. For more than 100 years, there was little need to **investigate** federal crimes because there were so few.

By the beginning of the 1900s, transportation became easier. Travel and crime between states became more common. Citizens wanted the federal government to be more powerful. As more federal laws were created, the attorney general had a hard time **enforcing** them. On July 26, 1908, Attorney General Charles Bonaparte created the Bureau of Investigation with a small team of "special agents."

FBI Responsibilities

1908	Train robberies · land **fraud** · copyright violations · crimes at sea · **forgery**
1910	White slavery
1918	Spies · military draft · deporting people
1919	Stealing cars
1920s	Gangsters · **Ku Klux Klan**
1932	Kidnapping
1934	Stolen property · **blackmail** · hurting or killing federal officers
1939	**Sabotage** · working against spies
1950s	More responsibility for gambling · bank robberies · anti-American groups
1960s	**civil rights** · **organized crime** · crimes on aircraft · sports bribery · safe streets
1970s	Corrupt organizations · local police killings · **terrorist** actions
1980s	Federal drug cases · terrorists attacking Americans abroad
1990s	Economic spying · health care fraud · stalking

Know It

FBI Names

1908   Bureau of Investigation

1932   United States Bureau of Investigation

1935   Federal Bureau of Investigation

At first, the FBI did not train special agents. The bosses were in Washington, D.C., but agents lived and worked in cities all over the United States. Many special agents became involved in local politics. Some even used their powers to help important people in their communities, instead of working to help the federal government. The American people saw FBI special agents doing good things like arresting enemies during World War I, but they also saw them involved in political **scandals**.

Charles Bonaparte

Charles Bonaparte was attorney general from 1906 to 1909. He was a grandnephew of Napoleon Bonaparte, the leader of France from 1804–1815. Bonaparte and President Theodore Roosevelt thought that a strong federal government could make **society** fair. They believed in using experts in subjects like science to help govern the country.

FBI Buildings Through The Years

1908

Headquarters of attorney general, Washington, D.C.

1917

Department of **Justice,** Washington, D.C.

1920s

Annex for Identification and Training, Washington, D.C.

1934

Department of Justice, Washington, D.C.

1940s

FBI Academy, Quantico, Virginia

1975

J. Edgar Hoover Building, Washington, D.C.

2000

FBI Laboratory, Quantico, Virginia

J. Edgar Hoover and the FBI

J. Edgar Hoover became director of the FBI in 1924, when he was 29 years old. He worked to clean up the image of the FBI. He fired anyone who seemed unfair or dishonest. He made rules stopping FBI agents from hitting people or drinking alcohol while working. He also stopped the FBI from giving people jobs just because they had important friends. Instead, Hoover started a system of grading how well FBI workers did their jobs. This helped to decide if they were ready to be **promoted.** Field offices were now inspected. All the FBI offices, wherever they were, had to follow the same rules.

In 1928, Hoover set up the first standard training course for all new special agents. He created the Identification Division, the first national collection of fingerprints. The FBI Laboratory opened, and the FBI National Police Academy helped train police officers from all over the country.

Gangsters

Most gangsters in the 1930s made and sold alcohol illegally. But the Department of the Treasury was in charge of **investigating** these crimes. If the FBI wanted to work on these crimes, it first had to find other laws that gangsters had broken. Al Capone, one of the most dangerous and powerful gangsters, broke the law by refusing to be a witness in a trial. This allowed the FBI to investigate him.

The FBI Identification Division had more than 800,000 fingerprints when it started in 1924. These were kept in files that had to be searched by hand.

By 1933, the FBI was a success with many Americans. Radio shows, movies, and newspaper and magazine stories told about the work of FBI special agents. These agents became known as G-Men, or government men. They were heroes to many people. Hoover had helped make the FBI an agency that citizens trusted and respected.

During World War II (1939–1945), the FBI worked to keep enemies from spying on the U.S. During the 1950s, many Americans believed in the threat of **communism**. FBI special agents investigated communist organizations and people they thought were communist spies. They caught some spies who were stealing secrets about the atom bomb. However, many people think the FBI went too far. They say that people's lives were hurt when they were wrongly accused of being communists.

Senator Joseph McCarthy was in charge of investigating people accused of being communists in the 1950s. He received stacks of letters both accusing people and saying they were innocent.

Know It

FBI Special Agents
were first allowed to carry guns and make arrests in 1934.

FBI Employees

Year	Special Agents	Support Staff
1908	9	25
1919	200	250
1924	441	209
1938	658	1,141
1945	4,000	9,000
1948	3,741	5,559
1958	5,977	7,217
1968	6,703	9,320
1978	8,000	11,000
1988	9,663	13,651
1998	11,453	16,498

Successes and Problems

In the 1960s, American soldiers were fighting a war in Vietnam. But many people did not want war. The FBI **investigated** thousands of people and groups that were **protesting** against the war. Again, many people thought the FBI went too far. They said that the FBI was bothering innocent people and not letting them give their opinions.

The National Crime Information Center was created at the FBI Headquarters in Washington, D.C., in 1967. Police and FBI special agents from all over the country could add information to this set of records and use it to help find criminals.

Know It

After Hoover

L. Patrick Gray, who was in charge of the FBI after J. Edgar Hoover, let women become special agents for the first time since the 1920s.

J. Edgar Hoover made a number of important arrests personally. He often talked with reporters about the FBI's successes. When he died in 1972, after nearly 48 years as the director of the FBI, he was very popular with Americans. But in 1975, the U.S. Senate began to study the way the FBI did its investigations. The Senate found that the FBI often used illegal methods.

In 1936, J. Edgar Hoover made sure he was the one to arrest Alvin "Creepy" Karpis (on the right). Karpis was a bank robber who had sent Hoover threatening letters.

FBI special agents had illegally **bugged** people's telephones and rooms. They had bothered people without good reasons. The FBI apologized for anything it had done wrong in the past. It made new rules for how it would behave in the future.

In the 1980s, the FBI dealt with many cases of **fraud,** spying, and illegal drugs. But after the **Cold War** ended in the early 1990s, the FBI turned its focus to violent crimes and crimes in people's homes. The FBI is always developing new ways to collect and share information. This helps to identify and stop criminals.

In 1971, the FBI arrested six members of the **Klu Klux Klan.** The men were planning to bomb school buses because they didn't think African-American and white children should go to school together. These weapons were found in their homes.

In 1964, Martin Luther King, Jr., went to see J. Edgar Hoover at the FBI. King didn't think the FBI was working hard enough to protect **civil rights.** Hoover thought King was a **communist.**

On File

The FBI holds a huge amount of information about most Americans. Even people who are not criminals have FBI files that include their driving records, phone records, and more. The Freedom of Information Act of 1966 states that everyone can see their FBI files. The Privacy Act of 1974 lets citizens correct or destroy records that are wrong.

The Structure of the FBI

This is the Department of Justice Building in Washington, D.C.

Each new U.S. president picks a **cabinet** to advise him or her. One of the cabinet members is the attorney general, who is in charge of the Department of **Justice**. With each new president, a new attorney general is picked. The FBI is part of the DOJ. The president also picks someone to be in charge of the FBI. An FBI director may hold the job for up to ten years, even with a different president in office. After ten years, the president must pick a new director.

FBI Headquarters is in the J. Edgar Hoover Building in Washington, D.C.

The FBI Headquarters in Washington, D.C., is known as FBIHQ. It's in the J. Edgar Hoover Building in downtown Washington. Inside FBIHQ are offices for the divisions that support the FBI's **investigations.** FBIHQ also has offices for other FBI divisions, such as for the lawyers in the Office of General Counsel. The FBI Academy is nearby, in Quantico, Virginia.

The FBI Academy is in Quantico, Virginia.

The Chicago field office is in the Everett Dirksen **Federal** Building.

This resident agency is in Rolling Meadows, Illinois.

This legal attaché office is in the U.S. embassy in Paris, France.

Special agents throughout the United States, or "in the field," handle the major investigations. At the moment, there are 56 field offices. Most field offices are in large, important cities. This is also where most crimes take place. Field offices are in charge of smaller offices in smaller cities and towns. These are called resident agencies. They may have one person working there or dozens, depending on how many are needed. Resident agencies can move, depending on where they are needed.

International Agents

Some crimes can cause problems in more than one country. Criminals can also travel to other countries. This is why there are FBI field agents in foreign countries. They work in the U.S. **embassies** in those countries. These agents work with local and international police to solve crimes involving drugs, spying, **terrorism,** and money.

Visit to the Chicago Field Office

The FBI must be able to send agents anywhere in the United States within two hours of a call for help. To do this, there must be FBI offices all over the country. The 56 field offices help answer these calls. Resident agencies working under the field offices' leadership can also help.

The Chicago field office is the fourth largest in the U.S. More than 800 people work here. Most of the special agents work in one of 34 squads, or teams, that **investigate** specific crimes. A squad may focus on violent crimes or drug-related crimes. Others work against **terrorism.** Some of the squads are called task forces. They work with local **law enforcement** to solve crimes such as bank robberies and kidnappings. In a smaller field office, there would be fewer squads. Agents there would investigate many types of crimes.

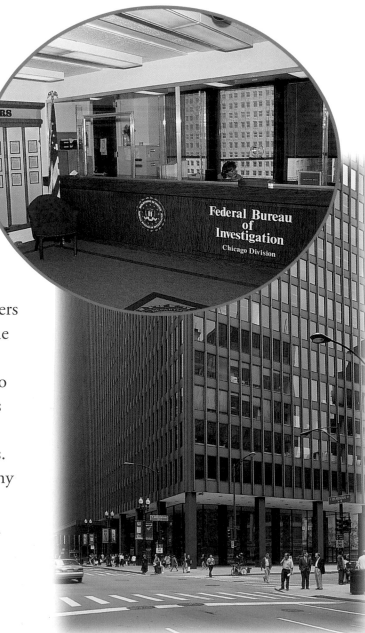

The FBI Chicago office is in downtown Chicago. It takes up three floors in the Everett McKinley Dirksen **Federal** Building. Smaller offices are in other nearby buildings and at O'Hare Airport, 15 miles (24 kilometers) away.

The Chicago office is usually quiet. Most special agents are out investigating crimes. When a crime is **committed**, the FBI sends an **Evidence** Response Team to the **crime scene.** The team investigates the scene, collects evidence, and stores it properly. The evidence can then be **analyzed** at the laboratory to see what clues it can give about the crime.

Computer and communications specialists work in the communications center. From this room, specialists can talk to agents throughout the Chicago area. **Surveillance** cameras located throughout the building are hooked up to video screens. The specialists can watch all entrances from this room.

Know It

The Chicago FBI field office handles about 200 bank robberies a year. It also arrests more than 200 violent criminals a year.

Special agents in the Chicago office use special devices to investigate crimes and people. Phone **bugs,** like this one from the 1960s, are still used. However, they are now much better!

Legal Attaché Offices

Crime doesn't stop at the United States borders. Spies, **terrorists**, drug dealers, and members of **organized crime** can **commit** crimes everywhere. They and their crimes can hurt people, governments, and businesses in many other countries. To solve these types of crimes, the FBI's Legal Attaché Program works in 52 countries. All FBI field offices in the U.S. can ask legal attaché offices for help. Much of the legal attachés' work is finding criminals who have left the U.S. for other countries.

Special agents called legal attachés work with another country's police. They train police officers to use the newest and best weapons. They teach new crime-solving ideas. Legal attachés also share information about criminals. When legal attachés need to **investigate** a clue in a foreign country, the local police help them. The legal attachés also work to keep foreign criminals from going to the United States.

Two U.S. **embassies** in Africa were bombed in 1998. The legal attachés from nearby countries were the first FBI agents to get to the scenes. They helped keep more people from getting hurt. They also started the investigation only hours after the bombs went off. The sooner an investigation starts, the better the chances are of finding the people who did it.

The FBI helped investigate the bombing of the United States embassy in Nairobi, Kenya, in 1998.

The FBI thought it was a very smart idea to have agents get to the crime scene so quickly. They started a new U.S.-based team especially for flying to a **crime scene** soon after the legal attaché arrives.

The Legal Attaché Program is run by the International Operations branch of the FBI. This branch works with U.S. and international police and governments on other things, too. One of its most important jobs is making sure police and other **law enforcement** people cooperate and help each other.

This legal attaché office in London, England, is located inside the United States embassy.

Legal Attaché Beginnings

The Legal Attaché Program began in 1940 with the Special Investigative Service, or SIS. The SIS worked in South America to get information about United States enemies during World War II. By the end of the 1940s, there were legal attaché offices in Ottawa, Canada; London, England; Paris, France; and Madrid, Spain.

Working for the FBI

There are two kinds of jobs with the FBI—special agents and professional support. Special agents **investigate** crimes. Professional support workers do other special jobs. These can include **analyzing evidence**, programming computers, taking photographs, and building models.

Could You Be a Special Agent?

Must be:
- U.S. citizen
- Aged 23–37

Must have:
- College degree
- Good vision
- Driver's license

Also good to have:
- Law degree
- Accountancy degree

Must not:
- Do drugs
- Be color-blind

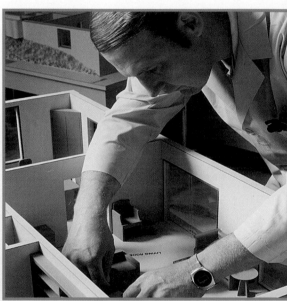

Could You Be in Professional Support?

Must be:
- U.S. citizen

Must have:
- completed high school

Also good to have:
- Specialized skills for specific jobs

Know It

While William H. Webster was FBI director from 1978 to 1987, the number of female special agents rose from 147 to 787, Hispanic agents from 173 to 400, and African-American agents from 185 to 393.

New agents practice their driving skills in special skid cars.

People who want to work for the FBI first go to a nearby field office. FBI officials have **applicants** go through many tests, such as lie detector and drug tests. They talk with the applicants' friends, neighbors, teachers, and bosses. FBI employees must be very honest. The FBI wants to know as much as possible about people before they are hired. The office in charge of jobs at FBIHQ makes the final decisions.

Special Agents

A new special agent is given a gun, a badge, a laptop computer, and papers saying he or she is a special agent.

New special agents go to school at the FBI Academy for sixteen weeks. They learn about handling guns, defending themselves, driving in special ways, and staying healthy. They learn how to think like an investigator does. They learn about laws and how to investigate crimes. When they start working, their first two years on the job are called probation. During this time, they learn more. Even when they finish probation, they still go back to school every so often to learn new ways to investigate and solve crimes.

Special agents often move to field offices. They can get **promoted** to leadership jobs if they do well. Most professional support workers stay in the same place. They do not move to new offices like special agents. They can change the type of job they do or get promoted doing the same kind of job.

The Training Division

The Training Division works with FBI special agents and police all over the world. Workers in this division teach others about **investigating** crimes and using the law. Classes are held at the FBI Academy. The learning takes place in school and during real investigations.

The FBI Academy in Quantico, Virginia

Special agents must learn how to control dangerous criminals.

How Much Training?

New Special Agents

- Must spend sixteen weeks at the FBI Academy

State or Local Police Officers

- Officers train for eleven weeks at the FBI Academy, learning investigation and leadership skills

- Chiefs of large police forces train for fifteen days at the Academy

- Officers in medium-sized forces must train for two weeks, learning about crimes and criminals

- Officers also take classes at the Academy and in police schools, learning more about guns, how criminals think, **DNA** analysis, computer crimes, bombs, and fingerprints.

The FBI Academy also is where the National Center for the **Analysis** of Violent Crime is located. Most police forces don't see many violent crimes. So the center has collected information about these kinds of crimes and criminals. It gives police help and training when they need it.

Physical Training

Special agents have to be in shape. Part of their training is regular exercise. They have to be able to do at least 20 pull-ups, 100 sit-ups, 50 push-ups, and run a mile (1.6 kilometers) in 7 minutes.

Know It

Practicing Street Skills

The FBI Academy built a fake town called Hogan's Alley. Trainees can practice catching criminals there, with actors playing the criminals.

Part of the training for special agents takes place in classrooms.

What Kind of Training?

FBI Agents or Police Officers:
- Must learn street survival training to help when investigating violent criminals and dangerous situations

FBI Agents or International Police Officers:
- Have on the job training during real investigations, such as bombings or bank **fraud**

International Police Officers:
- Train for one to two weeks in the In-Country Training Program, learning police skills
- Eight weeks at the International **Law Enforcement** Academy in either Budapest, Hungary, or Bangkok, Thailand.

The Criminal Investigative Division

CRIMINAL INVESTIGATIVE DIVISION

The Criminal **Investigative** Division of the FBI is in charge of finding the people who **commit** most of the crimes that the FBI investigates. This division investigates kidnappings, murders, bank robberies, and Internet crimes.

Investigating criminals and serious crimes is a team effort. The people who work at FBIHQ study what types of crimes are problems across the whole country. They help start new programs to try to solve problems like gang violence and crimes against children on the Internet. But they also let the field offices make decisions about how best to tackle tough local crime problems.

The Safe Streets program is a good example of how the FBI works. Officials at FBIHQ created the program but let citizens throughout the United States decide how to use it in their communities. Workers in field offices work with local **law enforcement** officers to create teams of experts. Together, they decide what the worst problems are in their communities. Teams make plans for how best to solve these problems. They work together to use their different skills in the best way possible. Now all but two of the field offices have Safe Streets groups. The FBI also started a Safe Trails program on Native American lands. It works in much the same way as the Safe Streets program.

Know It

The Violent Crimes and Major Offenders Section is part of the Criminal Investigative Division.

The section chief (on the right) and the assistant section chief of the Violent Crimes and Major Offenders Section meet often. They discuss how the division is working.

The leaders in the Criminal Investigative Division try to get **Congress** to pass laws that help solve crimes. For example, as the Internet became more popular, Internet crimes began to increase. The FBI now works with Internet companies and Congress to help catch criminals.

The people at FBIHQ also have to approve the field offices' plans for **undercover** work. If an undercover operation lasts longer than six months, it is reviewed at FBIHQ. The leaders at FBIHQ meet with people in the Department of **Justice** every two weeks. They look at all the operations that are under way and the rules they are following.

The Ten Most Wanted Fugitives program is run by the Violent Crimes and Major Offenders Section. The people at FBIHQ run the list. The field offices do the investigations and make arrests.

A Closer Look: A Computer Squad

As societies change, the types of crimes change as well. New inventions or machines change the way criminals work. Some criminals now use computers to steal money or information.

Some large FBI field offices now have special groups of agents who **investigate** computer crimes. Computer crimes include breaking into computer systems, removing or changing information on computers, making illegal copies of computer software, **committing** Internet **fraud**, and purposely creating and sending **computer viruses**. Computer crime squads also investigate stolen credit card numbers and people who illegally trade those numbers on the Internet.

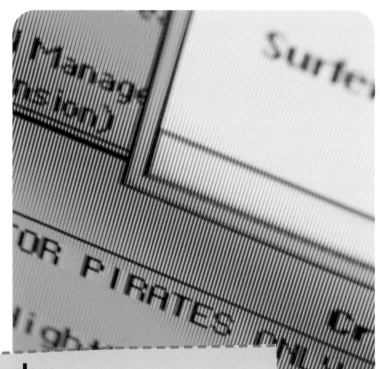

Computer Criminals

Hackers are people who use their computers to "break into" computer systems for fun and to prove how smart they are. Hackers usually try to steal or damage information.

Crackers are people who break into computer systems to steal, change, or destroy information.

Phreakers are people who use telephone systems to steal or get free telephone service.

Know It

Internet Advice for Kids

✔ Never give out personal information.

✔ Never trade Internet account numbers.

✔ Never open an e-mail or a file from someone you do not know.

Much of the work that computer squad special agents do involves working on a computer. They look at phone records of when criminals logged onto the Internet, and they read e-mails. These computer "records" are like fingerprints—they can tell when and where a person may have used his or her computer to commit a crime.

Often, special agents have to take apart computers to get important information. By opening up a computer, these experts are able to recover information or **evidence** that a criminal tried to destroy.

This special agent uses several computers to solve crimes.

The Laboratory Division

The place a crime is committed is called the **crime scene.** At all crime scenes, **evidence** is left behind. Evidence can be fingerprints, hair, bullets, or bits of fabric from clothes. Evidence is one of the most useful tools for people **investigating** crimes. But it has to be collected carefully. Scientists have to **analyze** evidence to learn about the crime. These scientists are called examiners. Examiners go to crime scenes to collect evidence. Sometimes they **testify** in court about the evidence they examine.

The FBI's Laboratory does detailed analysis. Lab workers there also teach other **law enforcement** workers how to collect and analyze evidence.

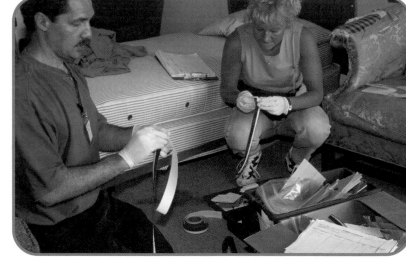

These examiners are collecting evidence at a crime scene.

Who is it?

FBI scientists can recreate a person's face from just a skull. A picture of the skull is scanned into a computer. Then markers are put at different places to show how thick the flesh should be. Pictures of different parts of faces are put in place. Then another scientist checks that the face seems right for the bones underneath and makes final changes.

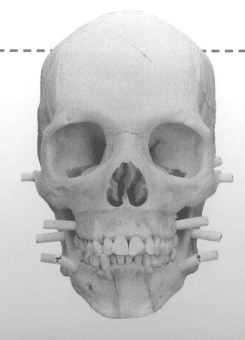

Laboratory analysis is not all about evidence. Video recorders at the laboratory run 24 hours a day, 7 days a week, taping television shows. They do this because sometimes criminals or victims talk about TV programs. The FBI has to know about them, too.

Often, the FBI is asked to find missing people. These people may be criminals or citizens who have disappeared. Some of these missing people haven't been seen in many years. Experts make pictures of how a person might look as he or she gets older. They start with what the young person looks like. Then they make the lines in the face look deeper, the skin less tight, and the color of the skin a bit different. They try to copy what happens when a person gets older. The pictures often look very much like the real person!

Know It
Collecting Evidence
The Oklahoma City bombing in 1995 produced more than 7,000 pounds of evidence for the FBI Laboratory to analyze.

FBI Labs
The FBI Laboratory never refuses a case. Any law enforcement office in the country can send in evidence to be analyzed for free.

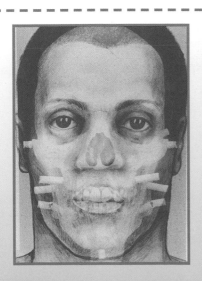
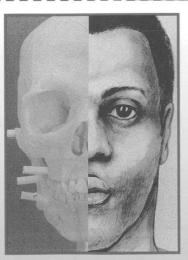
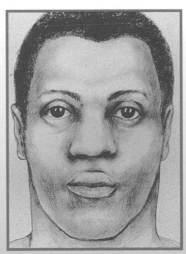

A Closer Look: A Trace Evidence Unit

Trace Evidence

Trace evidence can be left behind in many ways:

✔ Clothing can get hooked on something as a person leaves through a broken window.

✔ A bed sheet can be used to tie up a person.

✔ Feathers can come out of a coat.

✔ Hair from a bank robber's head can be left on a mask found at a crime scene.

All **crime scenes** are different. When the police or FBI get there, they often don't know what happened. They learn about what may have happened by studying the **evidence.** Police officers and special agents must examine the scene very carefully. Then they collect evidence to send to the lab to be **analyzed.** Some evidence is easy to lose because it is very small. This is called trace evidence. A special unit at the FBI Laboratory analyzes trace evidence.

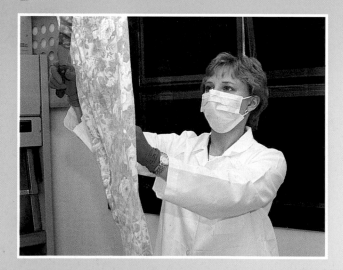

A piece of clothing may have hairs or **fibers** from other clothing on it. An FBI worker scrapes it with a tool until everything has fallen onto the paper below. Then the evidence is gathered into a small clear dish and labeled.

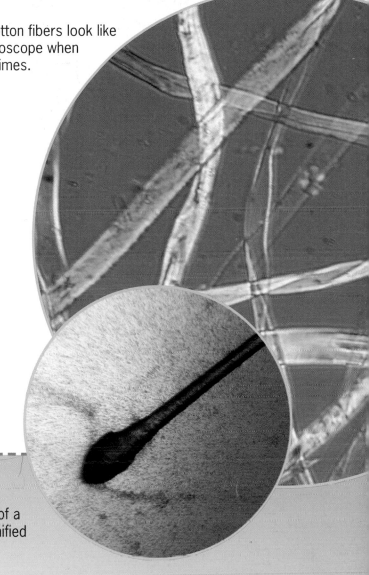

This is what cotton fibers look like through a microscope when magnified 80 times.

The person in charge of the trace evidence unit often starts out as a technician. He or she might work as a special agent and examiner before taking charge of the unit. The trace evidence unit is one of the busiest units in the FBI. This unit handles most of the cases that the FBI Laboratory **investigates.** It sees the evidence before any other unit does, to make sure nothing tiny is missed.

This is a picture of a human hair magnified 200 times.

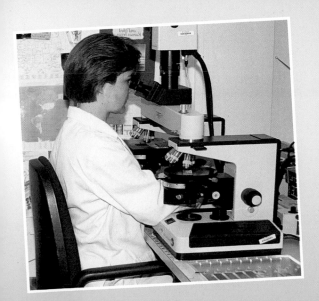

Next, the evidence is put onto a glass slide. A scientist called an examiner puts it under a microscope. The examiner looks to see if the evidence can be helpful. This examiner is looking at a fiber found at a bank robbery. If it is from the torn shirt of a person who said he wasn't there, she can use it to prove that he was lying and was indeed there. Examiners analyze hair, fibers, ropes, feathers, and wood.

A Closer Look: DNA Analysis Unit

DNA is a chemical code that tells a body how all of its parts should be made. People inherit DNA from their parents. There are two kinds of DNA. One kind, from blood or **saliva,** is **unique** for each person in the world. That means that no one else has the same DNA.

The other kind comes from hair, bones, and teeth. It is inherited from a person's mother. This kind of DNA is unique to anyone related to that mother—but that can be a lot of people. This kind of DNA match is still useful because it narrows down the number of possible suspects. Scientists work in the DNA Analysis Unit at the FBI Laboratory. They learn about new ways to use DNA in FBI **investigations.**

The FBI uses DNA to prove that a person was at a certain place or involved in a crime. The DNA found at the scene of a crime can be compared to the DNA from suspects. If the samples match, then the FBI can solve the case.

Sometimes a body is found and it can't be identified. DNA from the body can be compared to the DNA from missing persons. A match can help the FBI figure out the name of the found body. Sometimes criminals are caught, or innocent people set free, because of DNA **evidence** collected many years ago. Now there are new scientific techniques. The old DNA can finally be tested.

Know It

DNA

DNA samples will last thousands of years if they are kept away from the sun. This means even ancient bones can be checked.

How DNA Is Analyzed

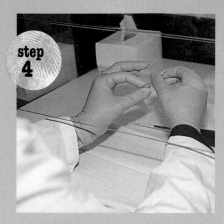

1. DNA evidence is collected at a **crime scene**. It is stored in paper bags to keep it in the dark.

2. A DNA sample is taken from a suspect. The best way is by rubbing a cotton swab against the inside of the suspect's cheek.

3. An FBI examiner unwraps the evidence and makes notes on how the package and the evidence look.

4. The DNA is prepared by taking a small piece of it and putting it in a tiny dish with chemicals. Then it is ground up. It is left to sit until the DNA is released. Finally, the DNA is washed so all the other cell material is taken away.

5. Chemicals are added to the tiny amount of clean DNA, and it is put into a machine. The DNA copies itself many times, until there is a large amount of the same DNA.

6. The DNA goes onto glass plates that are put into a typing machine. As the liquid DNA runs across the plates, the computer records the DNA information.

7. An examiner looks at the DNA information from the evidence and from the sample on the computer. Sometimes examiners check evidence against the FBI's huge **database** of DNA. The database includes samples from all the people **convicted** of violent crimes, plus all missing persons. The examiner searches for the specific places where DNA is the same and different to see if the samples match.

Criminal Justice Information Services Division

Crime **investigations** around the country provide much useful information. When criminals are arrested, their fingerprints are taken. Fingerprints are useful for identification, even when a person is not a criminal. In some states, people are fingerprinted when they get a driver's license. Some children are fingerprinted at school or by their parents in case the children ever get lost. Each criminal also gets a **criminal record.** This record tells about the person and describes the types of crimes he or she **committed.** Fingerprints and criminal records can be very helpful to **law enforcement** workers. However, this information needs to be kept in a place where everyone who needs it will know where and how to get it.

Know It

The Criminal Justice Information Services Division gets more than 37,000 new fingerprints every day!

This is the main complex of the Criminal Justice Information Services Division in West Virginia.

This is a
fingerprint card.

RIGHT HAND

2. Index Finger | 3. Middle Finger

LEFT HAND

7. Index Finger | 8. Middle Finger

The FBI's Criminal **Justice** Information Services Division, or CJIS, stores this valuable information. There is so much information that the CJIS has its own building in West Virginia.

The CJIS's giant computer **database** of fingerprint records has more than 250 million fingerprints. Police forces around the U.S. use the database. They can match fingerprints to criminal records and names. Fingerprints can also be used to identify bodies.

Police forces can send fingerprints to the FBI electronically. The database then searches for a match. Usually it takes less than two hours to do a search.

Every person who wants to buy a gun must first complete this NICS form.

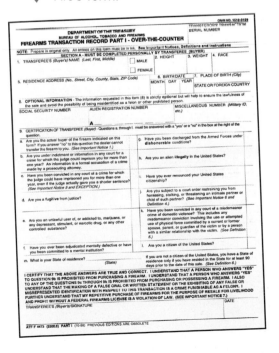

The CJIS is also in charge of the National Instant Check System, or NICS. U.S. citizens who want to buy guns must first be approved by the FBI. People who have committed crimes or who are trying to escape arrest are not allowed to buy guns. The NICS checks the FBI criminal records databases. It can let gun sellers know if a person is allowed to buy a gun or not. Since starting in 1998, the NICS has checked the names of more than thirteen million gun buyers. More than 3,200 gun buyers were wanted by police. Some were arrested after they tried to buy a gun. Because of these background checks, many crimes may have been prevented.

A Closer Look: The Latent Print Unit

This is a detailed picture of a fingerprint.

The FBI's **Latent Print** Unit works with tiny pieces of latent prints. These can help solve crimes and identify disaster victims. A latent print, such as a fingerprint, is made by the ridged skin on a person's fingers, hands, and feet. An expert can look at these prints and tell who left them and sometimes even what the person was doing. The FBI's Latent Print Unit works for free, so even small police stations can use this expensive and effective technology. Experts in the Latent Print Unit teach police officers and other FBI special agents how to collect **crime scene evidence** without ruining the prints.

Taking prints is usually very easy. All that is needed is ink and a special card with spaces for a person's fingerprints and palm prints. However, criminals do not carry around this equipment when they are **committing** crimes!

Fingerprint cards have not changed much since this one was made for "Pretty Boy" Floyd, a dangerous criminal in the 1930s.

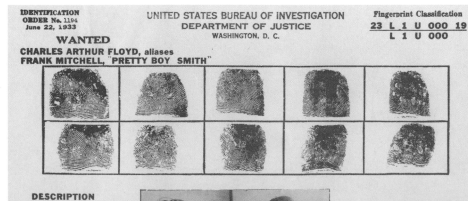

Special glues can find invisible prints on hard objects, such as this gun.

Experts often use special kinds of light to show invisible prints.

But criminals still leave fingerprints behind, even if they don't think they do. Fingerprints can be left behind when a person touches things. Sometimes these prints are easy to see, like when a person's hand was covered in paint or blood. However, most latent prints can't be seen without help from special equipment. These types of prints are discovered by several different methods. A special powder can be dusted onto objects to reveal fingerprints. Once the prints are found, sticky tape is used to lift the prints from the object.

Latent print experts do much of their work as part of the Disaster Squad. This group has identified thousands of people who have died in disasters, like airplane crashes and bombings. Forty members of the Disaster Squad are always ready to fly to anywhere in the world to help when needed. Disaster Squad workers use whatever they can—fingers, hands, footprints, teeth, and even **DNA**—to identify the bodies of victims.

Body parts, such as this cut-off finger, help to identify victims by their fingerprints.

A Closer Look: Adopt-A-School

Special Agent Barbara Wallace, known as Bobi, is in charge of the Community Outreach Unit. This is part of the Office of Public and Congressional Affairs, based at FBIHQ in Washington, D.C. When Bobi started in 1989, she wanted to get FBI agents involved in the everyday lives of children.

Bobi developed the Adopt-A-School Program. Special agents work in many different ways. Some schools need special agents as **tutors** to help students learn difficult subjects. Some schools ask for special agents to work with violent students or those who are using drugs. They help the children learn self-respect and teach them how to make better decisions in the future.

Special Agent Bobi Wallace talks to the new junior special agents at their graduation ceremony.

Leaders from the FBI and local school district give the junior special agents their badges.

Some schools ask FBI agents to teach students about what it is like to work for the FBI. This is called the Junior Special Agent Program. Students in this program work on projects that help them learn about respect and self-control. They learn about the United States and the freedoms its citizens have. More than 9,000 special agents help across the country.

When the students have earned their junior special agent badges, they have a graduation ceremony at the FBI office. As Bobi said at one graduation, "This is the junior special agents' day to shine. They know the FBI backs them. They are now part of the FBI family."

However they work with a school, special agents are helping the students learn to reach goals. The special agents talk about the importance of a good education. Their message is, "Dream it, plan it, do it." In ten years, more than 750,000 students have become junior special agents.

The Adopt-A-School Program is helping more good people to graduate. Special Agent Bobi Wallace hopes some of them will choose to work for the FBI in the future.

This student won first place for his poster about what being a junior special agent means to him. He thinks that being a junior special agent will help him reach his goal of being a family services lawyer.

The FBI Reaching Out

The FBI Community Outreach Unit works with citizens in many ways. It leads the FBI Citizens' Academy, an eight-week program for business and community leaders. FBI field offices also work with citizens in communities. Citizens learn about **law enforcement,** crime solving, and how the FBI works. Citizens and FBI agents also talk about how to work together to make communities safer.

These women were some of the sixteen people who participated in Newark, N.J.'s first Citizens' Academy community program in 1999.

The FBI works closely with police forces all over the world to prevent and solve crimes. Since 1990, the International Association of Chiefs of Police has worked with the FBI. Together, they try to think of new ways to stop gangs, drugs, and violence by working with young people and law enforcement around the world. They try to prevent crime by making young people who might **commit** crimes their partners instead of their enemies. Together they can learn to respect and help each other.

Your Code Word

The FBI says you and your parents should share a secret code word. Then, if a stranger says that your parents want you to go somewhere with him or her, he or she should also tell you the code word. If he or she doesn't know the code word, run away as fast as possible!

The FBI has a Strategic Information Operations Center used after **terrorist** attacks. A similar **counterterrorism** center is set up at the CIA. Workers from many **government agencies** work at both centers. Within minutes of a terrorist attack, teams get to work.

The Detroit, Michigan, FBI field office had a Red Ribbon Day parade with a local school. Students promised to stay drug-free. They made posters about not doing drugs and marched through their neighborhood.

Working Together

The FBI works with other government agencies as well. The FBI and the Environmental Protection Agency (EPA) worked together to catch a company breaking the law. In January 2000, Chemetco, a copper business in Illinois, said it had poured chemicals into a lake. The chemicals lay on the lake bed, poisoning animals, plants, and people. The EPA knew Chemetco had poured chemicals into the lake in 1986, but Chemetco said it had done it by accident, and only that one time. The FBI and the EPA went to the company's plant and **investigated.** They also read through

Scientists from the EPA help the FBI catch people who break the law. This scientist is checking for water pollution.

company papers. They discovered that a secret pipe had been used for about ten years to dump chemicals into the lake. The company's owner had ordered the pipe to be built. Chemetco was fined almost a million dollars.

Always Advancing

FBI leaders are always planning for the future. They know that their work is very important to the country. Finding **terrorists** after they attack has become the most important work the FBI does. Every day, it is very important to keep foreign spies, terrorists, and criminals from stealing military or other secrets or weapons, or from **hacking** into important computers. Stopping crimes that hurt large numbers of people, such as selling illegal drugs, is the next most important job.

Terrorist Caught

Terrorist Ramzi Yousef used secret codes to protect the information on his computer that told about his 1993 bombing of the World Trade Center in New York City.

Mobile Labs

Getting and **analyzing evidence** at the scene of a terrorist crime is better than sending it to the FBI Laboratory in Washington, D.C. The FBI is working on small laboratory kits that can be taken to and used at **crime scenes.**

Even when it plans for the future, the FBI remembers its past. This statue in the courtyard at headquarters is in memory of FBI agents who were killed while on duty.

FIDELITY · BRAVERY · INTEGRITY

Finally, the FBI continues to improve the ways it **investigates** crimes against common citizens. New, more powerful computers help special **databases** talk to each other. Soon every special agent will be able to ask all the databases questions from wherever he or she is. Police forces around the country will also be able to use the databases to help in their work.

Mobile Information

A new system lets police send a single fingerprint to the FBI from a police car. The FBI quickly checks who the person is and if he or she has a **criminal record.** Photos of suspects can also be sent and printed right in the car.

The new powerful computers that help the FBI solve crimes can be used against them, however. Criminals can use secret codes to scramble information so it's difficult to read or understand. Computers can store a large amount of important information on a small disk that can easily be moved and hidden.

Specialized Data

Some database systems help make connections between crimes, like **serial murders** or shootings. One database matches **DNA** from criminals and unsolved crimes all over the country. Another stores information about the bullets used in shootings throughout large areas.

The FBI will always work to keep ahead of the new ways criminals break the law. Special agents will find new ways to bring criminals to **justice.**

Sometimes the best science is very simple. These planters each weigh one ton. They stop vehicles from getting too close to the FBIHQ building and damaging it.

FBI Organization

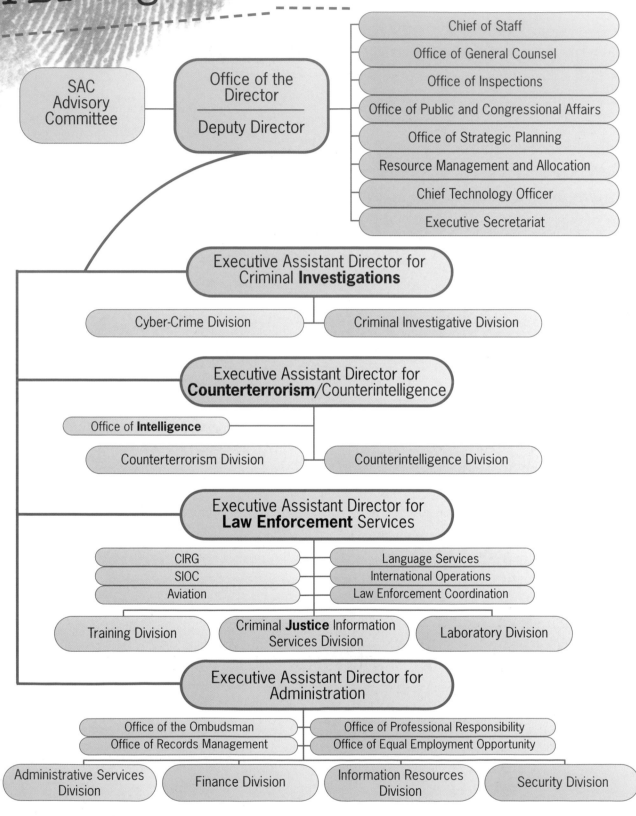

SAC Advisory Committee

Office of the Director
Deputy Director

- Chief of Staff
- Office of General Counsel
- Office of Inspections
- Office of Public and Congressional Affairs
- Office of Strategic Planning
- Resource Management and Allocation
- Chief Technology Officer
- Executive Secretariat

Executive Assistant Director for Criminal Investigations

- Cyber-Crime Division
- Criminal Investigative Division

Executive Assistant Director for Counterterrorism/Counterintelligence

- Office of Intelligence
- Counterterrorism Division
- Counterintelligence Division

Executive Assistant Director for Law Enforcement Services

- CIRG
- SIOC
- Aviation
- Language Services
- International Operations
- Law Enforcement Coordination
- Training Division
- Criminal Justice Information Services Division
- Laboratory Division

Executive Assistant Director for Administration

- Office of the Ombudsman
- Office of Records Management
- Office of Professional Responsibility
- Office of Equal Employment Opportunity
- Administrative Services Division
- Finance Division
- Information Resources Division
- Security Division

More Books to Read

Balcavage, Dynise. *The Federal Bureau of Investigation.* Broomall, Penn.: Chelsea House, 2000.

Foltz Jones, Charlotte. *Fingerprints and Talking Bones: How Real-Life Crimes Are Solved.* New York: Delacorte Press, 1997.

Heath, David. *Crime Lab Technician.* Mankato, Minn.: Capstone Publishing Company, 1999.

Kronenwetter, Michael. *The FBI and Law Enforcement Agencies of the United States.* Berkeley Heights, N.J.: Enslow Publishers, 1997.

Lane, Brian. *Crime and Detection.* New York: Dorling Kindersley Publishing, Incorporated, 2000.

Contacting the FBI

Federal Bureau of Investigation
J. Edgar Hoover Building
935 Pennsylvania Avenue, N.W.
Washington, D.C. 20535-0001
(202) 324-3000

Federal Bureau of Investigation
Suite 1700, FOB
11000 Wilshire Boulevard
Los Angeles, California 90024-3672
(310) 477-6565

Federal Bureau of Investigation
Room 905
E. M. Dirksen Federal Office Building
219 South Dearborn Street
Chicago, Illinois 60604-1702
(312) 431-1333

Federal Bureau of Investigation
26 Federal Plaza, 23rd Floor
New York, New York 10278-0004
(212) 384-1000

Glossary

analyze to look at and study something very carefully

applicant person who asks a company or organization for a job

blackmail crime of threatening to tell something harmful about someone unless the person pays money

bug small microphone device; or to hide a microphone to record conversations secretly

cabinet group of people that gives the president advice

civil rights rights of all citizens—no matter what race, religion, sex, or place of birth—guaranteed by the U.S. Constitution

Cold War time between the end of World War II in 1945 and the early 1990s when communist countries, led by the Soviet Union, were enemies of capitalist countries, led by the United States

commit to be responsible for doing something

communism political and economic system in which the government owns all factories and businesses

computer virus computer code that destroys or damages computers or information

Congress group of people who make the laws for the United States; includes the Senate and House of Representatives

convicted found guilty of a crime

counterterrorism work done to try to stop terrorism

crime scene location where a crime has been commited

criminal record file of papers that tells about a criminal, including his or her looks, names used, and types of crimes committed

database system that stores information in such a way that it can be used easily, usually on a computer

discrimination treating people in an unkind or unfair way

DNA chemical code in the human body that tells the body how all of its parts should be made

embassy group of workers sent by a country to represent it in another country. The building in which this group works is also called an embassy.

enforce to make sure laws are followed

evidence anything that is left behind after a crime or that helps to solve the crime

federal describing a union of states that share a government

fiber little piece of the thread or yarn that makes up a fabric or cloth

forgery false copy of something

fraud tricking someone to get money or a service

fugitive person on the run from something

government agency part of a government that gives a special kind of help

hacker person who illegally breaks into computers and computer systems by using a computer or other electronic methods

high-tech very complicated, using the latest and best technologies

hijack to take control of a vehicle by force

intelligence information about something important, usually secret

investigate to examine in detail to discover facts

justice being fair, upholding what is right according to laws

Ku Klux Klan secret group of white people that is against equal rights for African Americans

latent print mark made on a surface by a person's fingers, hands, or feet

law enforcement making sure citizens follow laws and protecting citizens from criminals; or groups of people who do these jobs

Mafia secret criminal group that began in Italy, on the island of Sicily

organized crime very large criminal activity by organized groups of criminals

promoted being rewarded with a job that usually pays more money and has more responsibility

prosecute to bring legal action against someone for a crime

protest to show disagreement with something, usually in a public place

sabotage destruction of property or resources by an enemy

saliva waterlike liquid in a person's mouth; also called spit

scandal problem that causes embarrassment or public disgrace

security risk threat to sensitive information or to people's safety

serial murders several murders committed by the same person, often in the same way

society people living together in a group, like a community or country, and sharing a way of life

surveillance watching someone closely

terrorism use of violence for political reasons

testify to be questioned by lawyers, judges, and others in a court of law

tutor person who teaches others, usually outside of a school

undercover hidden or secret

unique one of a kind

white-collar crime type of crime that is usually committed by businesspeople, often as they do their jobs

Index